WHEN GOD SAYS, "DROP IT!"

Chronicles of My Healing

DONNA MARTELLI

Trilogy Christian Publishers
A Wholly Owned Subsidiary of Trinity Broadcasting Network
2442 Michelle Drive
Tustin, CA 92780

Cover design by: Cornerstone Creative Solutions

For information, address Trilogy Christian Publishing
Rights Department, 2442 Michelle Drive, Tustin, Ca 92780.
Trilogy Christian Publishing/ TBN and colophon are trademarks of Trinity Broadcasting Network.

For information about special discounts for bulk purchases, please contact Trilogy Christian Publishing.

Manufactured in the United States of America

10 9 8 7 6 5 4 3 2 1

Library of Congress Cataloging-in-Publication Data is available.

ISBN 978-1-63769-182-3 (Print Book)
ISBN 978-1-63769-183-0 (ebook)

This book is dedicated to

Jesus, my Lord, my Savior, my Love, Who redeemed my life from destruction.

My husband, my caregiver by default, who lovingly stayed by my side and helped me through this time.

My pastor, who shepherds my soul.

My church family, who prayed in faith for me continually.

All who prayed and warred in the Spirit for my healing.

Contents

Acknowledgements

Cover Design: Del Bock
Editors: Del Bock, Donna Martelli
Photography: Del Bock, Janet Hunt, Paul Martelli, Nadine Egan, Donald Stanley

Preface

God speaks in many ways, often odd or funny. Sitting in my car waiting for my fitness client to open the gate to her condo, I randomly started adding all the numbers on my dashboard. Mind you; this is not a habit of mine, just an odd-ball thing to do, I guess. However, all of the numbers added to eight or a multiple of eight: mileage 2222, mpg 26.8, miles to go on tank 197, time 7:01!

8

Eight is the number of new beginnings. I did not know of anything new happening in my life, so I just noted the phenomenon, and I wondered if God was going to do something new. Could it be that He was letting me know in advance?

What was new? Nothing at that point. I loved my life, riding the vapor, running here, running there, sometimes physically, but always in my head. I worked as a dance and fitness instructor, a vocation God prepared me for and placed me into. I thoroughly enjoyed my work.

But that number 8 was in everything I read, heard, or saw. I mentioned it to a couple of Godly people, but mostly I pondered it in my heart. Then I saw it happen.

Introduction

You picked up this book, so you must be ready to stop fooling around and finally receive God's healing. What it comes down to, the bottom line is this: you have to believe that God will heal you, not just that He can heal you. Psalm 103 says that He forgives all our sin and heals all our diseases, among other wonderful things.

Only when we choose to make God's Word our standard can we begin to understand and believe that God wants us to be well. Then we can receive His healing.

God hears our prayers. Walk with me through my journey and experience the Lord's love with me. My prayer for you:

Father, I pray for everyone who hears or reads these words. May each be strengthened with might in their inner person. May each step closer to you and may their faith grow by leaps and bounds as they hear of the marvelous things that you have done in my life. Bless them, Father, and assure them that You will do the same for them. In Jesus' Name, amen.

Worn Out and Stressed Out

One evening while teaching my dance class, I saw a sliver of twinkling spots on a black velvet background as the room swayed around me. As I bent forward in a stretch, I was praying, *Lord, don't let me pass out!* My feet weren't going where I wanted them to go. Inwardly I was crying, *Lord, help me through this class, Lord, please hide these foibles from my students.* I don't think they noticed anything strange. At least, I hope not!

Attempting to balance turned into a new choreographic move, *Jesus, what is happening to me?* Though I knew He was with me, I felt He had let go of my hand. Had He? Of course, He had not, but I couldn't feel His presence.

Lord Jesus, where are You? I need You! Help! I felt like I was descending into a pit. I lacked the strength to climb out. It was terrifying. Has anything like this ever happened to you?

As a former professional ballerina and now a dance and fitness instructor, I am used to my body obeying what I tell it to do. What had happened here? I was baffled but, later on, with remarkable 20/20, hindsight I saw that I had stepped out of my assignment on this planet. How? It was a very gradual process of events and reactions to them that brought me to this point.

Many things can hinder us from receiving healing. God created us healthy, without illness or disease. These are outside forces that come against us. We have the power and the authority to kick them out, but sometimes things stop us from receiving.

My life was seriously out of whack. Balance in all parts of life is essential yet often challenging to achieve. Nature is our best example of balance:

light—dark
high—low
mountains—valley
hot—cold
sleeping—waking

Notice how they work together. If something is out of balance, it stresses both sides. Think about this: if your car is out of alignment, all sorts of other things go wrong. Your tires wear out, stuff in the engine shifts so that things touch that should not, and all kinds of other problems develop. Everything tries to right itself, but each part is forced to do a job that it was not created to do. It is a big mess!

As for me, I am a disciplined person, an ingrained trait that no doubt came from spending much of my life in a ballet studio. I learned to push past pain to achieve whatever I wanted my body to do.

Being a Type-A personality and carrying this discipline into everyday life became a snare to me.

1. I was overworked.
2. I stressed when things did not move along as I desired.
3. I placed a burden on myself that I was never intended to carry.
4. I pushed and pushed and pushed.

I was determined to become a great dancer from the sweet age of ten. My classical ballet study began with one class a week, and by my mid-teens, it had progressed to six days a week. During my senior year in high school, I danced many leading roles in major ballets, including Swan Lake, Ondine, and various original works. I was a big fish in the proverbial little pond.

What happened next was amazing in the way it transpired. I had won a trip to New York City as the Alabama Society of Arts and Letters talent competition winner. The New York trip was for the purpose of competing in nationals. I did not care about the national competition, but I went to every ballet school in the city. I even attended a professional audition just for the experience. In the end, I was selected as one of eight girls from over two hundred and fifty candidates to be a trainee in the Harkness Ballet of New York. After a summer intensive in Watch Hill, RI, I lived in New York City and attended Harkness House for Ballet Arts on a full-ride scholarship.

Within the first week of classes, all the trainees were whisked off to a doctor who would determine if we were physically capable of the task at hand. Every one of us was prescribed diet pills, which turned out to be none other than dynamite speed. This speed proved to be a pace-setter for me. It provided a fantastic do-it-all strength and drive, which I find appealing, even to this day. At Harkness House, I had the best teachers in the entire world. Besides classes in ballet and modern dance, we studied music theory, labanotation, character dance, choreography, anatomy, and other dance-related subjects. Seven months into the trainee program, I joined the Harkness Ballet Company, with whom I toured Europe and North Africa, dancing various parts in many ballets utilizing ballet, modern, and jazz dance techniques.

Years later, after a life of sin in which I tried everything else first, I met Jesus. In December 1980, I bowed my knee and acknowledged Jesus as my Lord and Savior. I accepted His payment for my sin: His precious blood, which He willingly shed for me on the cross of Calvary some 2000 years ago. I was immediately forgiven and free: His new creation, His child! My husband and I started attending an over-conservative church that taught that Christians don't dance. I didn't know any better, so I laid dance down. However, in church, I would see visions of choreography to hymns. I tried to push it out of my head, but it would not leave me alone.

In January 1988, Jesus baptized me with His precious Holy Spirit, and He gave me the power to be His witness. Furthermore, He had already given me the tool that He wanted me to use to be His witness. When I received the baptism of the Holy Spirit, I realized those visions of choreography were from Him. He gave dance back to me in a new and sanctified way. Now, I love teaching those who desire to dance for the Lord. Additionally, I became a certified personal trainer and certified Pilates instructor because of my passion for the healing aspects of dance and movement.

As for how I got to the point of illness, strife at home was a contributor, as it seemed my husband was always angry with me, which deflated my self-esteem. I tried to change myself to give him what he wanted, but then he would change what he wanted. He would tell me what I was thinking and be mad at what he incorrectly thought I thought. Indeed, this deserves another book someday, but for now, this will give you the idea. Jesus always goes before us, and He did smooth out our issues. If you have marital problems, please lay them down at the feet of Jesus. He knows how to deal with them. It is necessary for your healing.

From 2007–2014, I had a deep friendship with an amazing woman from work. We considered ourselves adopted sisters. Never having had a sister, I followed her lead. She leaned on me, and I leaned on her. We shared food, time, ideas, dreams, prayers, secrets; you name it. That is what sisters do, right? I loved her dearly. One day she didn't call me, then another and another. She cut me off. No texts, no calls, nothing! My little heart broke into a million pieces. "Lord, what have I done wrong?"

I learned this behavior is called ghosting. The following is from an article by Dr. Jennice Vilhauer.

Ghosting, for those of you who haven't yet experienced it, is having someone that you believe cares about you, whether it be a friend or someone you are dating, disappear from contact without any explanation at all. No phone call or email, not even a text. Ghosting isn't new—people have long done disappearing acts—but years ago this kind of behavior was considered limited to a certain type of scoundrel.

People who ghost are primarily focused on avoiding their own emotional discomfort and they aren't thinking about how it makes the other person feel.

One of the most insidious aspects of ghosting is that it doesn't just cause you to question the validity of the relationship you had, it causes you to question yourself. Why didn't I see this coming? How could I have been such a poor judge of character? What did I do to cause this? How do I protect myself from this ever happening again? This self-questioning is the result of basic psychological systems that are in place to monitor one's social standing and relay that information back to the person via feelings of self-worth and self-esteem. When a rejection occurs, your self-esteem can drop.

Ghosting is the ultimate use of the silent treatment, a tactic that has often been viewed by mental health professionals as a form of emotional cruelty. It essentially renders you powerless and leaves you with no opportunity to ask questions or be provided with information that would help you emotionally process the experience. It silences you and prevents you from expressing your emotions and being heard, which is important for maintaining your self-esteem. Regardless of the ghoster's intent, ghosting is a passive-aggressive interpersonal tactic that can leave bruises and scars.

When I confronted my friend, the reply I got was from a woman who was *not* the sister I knew so well. She had changed her attitude, and her reply was that she no longer had time for me. I took the rejection into my soul, spirit, and body. I was ill for several weeks because of this. Then, my anger fueled my strength. "Jesus, how can I survive this hurt?" Putting a name to rejection did help the pain subside, but I needed more than the facts. Only Jesus can heal this sort of profound emotional devastation. I thought about it way too much. Eventually, of course, I forgave her.

With fabulous hindsight again, I saw God's hand in what had transpired. I thank Him for that relationship, but it was time for a new thing. I was ready to move on.

Remember the 8s? They were manifesting all around me. My employer downsized and dissolved my position. One of my major, long time clients moved out of state. I lost all my email contacts. All this seemed to indicate the need for a reboot. "Now what, Lord?"

Acting logically, because I am a certified Pilates instructor and certified personal trainer, I decided to let area fitness clubs know of my availability. I felt drawn to a club whose marquee had sometimes displayed scriptures. A three-minute visit and a dropped off resume resulted in a phone call from the manager. That was the first, the last, and the only club I visited when looking for employment. "Lord, make it clear to me what You want here. Let me know Your geart on this." I told the owner and the manager about my past dance experience as a professional ballerina and instructor. They were excited and asked if I could teach barre classes. They had been praying for someone with my exact qualifications to come to them, and I had been praying for my new position to be one who would use my gifts and talents totally in what the Lord wanted for me. It was a dream come true. I entered my new position with the club as Director of Fitness Arts, a title conceived by my creative husband. Thank You, Lord!

I was totally in my niche. I created and taught a barre class program, hired and trained instructors, and introduced ballet for fitness to the club. It was all a perfect platform for sharing Jesus' love using the gifts and talents He has given to me for this purpose. I loved my work.

I hope this true story will inspire you and strengthen your faith in the power of prayer and the goodness of our God. He loves you and me!

Back to the fitness club: what happened?

The first year was superb, but I veered off track in several ways. Overworking and stressing caused unpleasant reactions in my body. My human ambition and drive have always been extraordinarily strong, a discipline I had ingrained in me during my life as a ballet dancer. Now, I was pushing past my boundaries as I was also entering the arena of pressure sales, which was not my thing.

I was ever so slightly taking pride in what I had done and not always giving credit to what the Lord had done. Why? It was because of what people would think. Hey, I sold more club memberships than anyone else one month. These two things put a big check in my spirit!

Additionally, I wanted others to push ahead at my pace and in my way. I wanted others to get it right, my way, again. I became sincerely and deeply grieved with issues at work or in others that were not perfect, in my opinion. I felt I was not allowed to use my gifts at work. My many creative ideas were ignored, or so I thought.

The pattern was evident. It was all about me, me, my, my, I, I! Just who is the Lord, here? Making it all about me makes an idol of me. We cannot worship the "me god". In the Word, we read that God is a jealous God, and He will not tolerate idols in our hearts. He knows all about you and me, and He is the Master at getting us to face ourselves and destroy those things that keep us from Him. That is an excellent thing because it proves we belong to Him.

I prayed, "Lord Jesus, I want Your wisdom and Your direction. I want only what You want."

God is faithful and true. He always answers our prayers. As I leaned to myself, He was letting me be His somewhat mischievous child. In His great love, He was watching and directing me, putting up boundaries I knew nothing of, and keeping His eye on me so I would not get into anything too dangerous.

I remember when my first son was two years old. He was innocent and inquisitive as all children are. He wanted to please me but was constantly checking out all sorts of things and getting into everything in sight. He did not know some things could hurt him or that they might not be right for him: this is how he learned. My eye was watchful, but I let him explore, always pulling him back from the brink of a harmful act. That is how I can best explain that the Lord was with me.

God sees me like this!

Think about it:

God gives every "good and perfect gift" (James 1:17). The problems only arise when we move out on our own to a place, an attitude, or a mindset that He did not ordain.

Obeying What You Hear?

> Do not merely listen to the word,
> and so deceive yourselves. Do what it
> says.
>
> James 1:22

Be sure of this: if you hear the Word of the Lord, whether logos, the written word, or rhema, the spoken word, get to it. God will keep bringing it back until you do, and maybe you will miss the blessing He has planned for you. He is such a good papa.

Like the little kid I am at heart, I tend to keep going until I drop. I am reminded of my two-year-old: discovering, learning, going from one thing to the next, until he literally drops in his tracks. I was at that place of exhaustion. Do not ever let it go this far. I love being busy, improving myself and everyone and everything around me. It's just who I am, and I enjoy it very much. But there comes a day when it is time to stop and rest. I do not like to rest, do you?

I had created a barre and ballet program and trained instructors to teach them according to the guidelines I had written. The program was established and growing. I felt ready for the next grand adventure.

"Lord, what do you want me to do next?" Expecting to hear about some epic new thing, I was unprepared for His answer. He gave me one simple word: "Stand." Huh?

In my spirit, I knew I should slow down, but what does it mean to stand? The Word says, "Therefore, put on the full armor of God, so that when the day of evil comes, you may be able to stand your ground, and after you have done everything, to stand" (Ephesians 6:13). According to the Strong's Concordance, one of the definitions of the word stand is, "To stop, stand still, stand immovable, stand firm as of the foundation of a building."

"Really, Lord, just stand?" I heard Him loudly and clearly, but I just kept on doing what I was doing. Warning: When we hear the instructive voice of the Lord and we do not obey it, there will be consequences. I heard but did not obey what the Lord spoke to me.

There were many excellent reasons not to stand. I knew God had called me to teach and train as I was doing. Yes, that was and is true, but He said at that particular time to *stand*. I stumbled at what He spoke to my heart. I had no concept of the meaning of what He meant by, *stand* and I had a sneaking suspicion that I didn't want to do it,

Throughout the days that followed, I kept on going as I had been, waiting for further direction from my Lord. I heard nothing from Him regarding what I should do next. Because I didn't obey Him when He told me to *stand*, He wasn't going to give me the marching orders I wanted. Instead, He spoke to me more firmly and said very plainly, "Halt!"

"But I thought You wanted me to do all of this!" He did, yes, but He was calling me at that particular time to slow down and rest. I did not obey this either. Warning: When we hear the instructive voice of the Lord and we do not obey it, there will be consequences. The consequence for me was an illness no doctor could identify. He warned me to stand and then halt, and when I did not do these two things, He made sure I did both of them. He allowed the consequence of my disobedience to run its course.

It is staggering to realize, had I obeyed "stand" and "halt" when I heard it, I would not have endured two and a half years of this illness, resulting in lost income, missed opportunities, and the deep, dark accompanying depression.

From my journal:

As I study Galatians 1, I am impressed that we humans naturally turn towards a different gospel: that of "Do it yourself." We naturally want to add to what He says by our own "Do it yourself" efforts and plans. It is not right.

Regarding my current little life situation, He is the One who is supposed to be doing it, not me. Labor, yes, in what He shows me, try to figure it out, no, that is leaning to my own understanding instead of trusting Him. Trying to do it, whatever good thing it may be, in our own way and trying to figure out what God is doing, is a return to the Law (bondage). It makes us a transgressor. Strong, isn't it?

But my God is totally good, and even though I was disobedient in applying His word to my life when I heard it, resulting in illness, He used it to teach me so much about healing, myself, and Himself. As always, Roman's 8:28, "And we know that all things work together for good to those who love God, to those who are the called according to His purpose."

"How Lord? All things, even this?" I couldn't see how He would use this for good. When you're in the middle of an illness, you must call in the troops to pray for you. Fortunately, I have a strong support system of prayer warriors who upheld me during this time. This support is only one reason why it is crucial to have a church family that believes in the Bible and accepts all of God's spiritual gifts. God desires this. You must have praying people you can go to. If you don't have them now, it's time to find some.

And now for the proverbial last straw: by attempting to work with fatigue and overtraining symptoms, and because I did not obey what the Lord told me to do, I opened the door for the enemy's attack. After a barre class, I was discussing Biblical truths with a client, and after a second client who had overheard our discussion approached me. While this was a private discussion between the first client and me, the second client called me aside and said directly to my face, "You know how much I love your class. But if this talk continues, I will not come back. I want to come here and work my body and not hear that. And furthermore, I believe there are many ways to God and Jesus isn't the only way." The door of her heart was slammed shut, and she heard nothing but her own words. She canceled her membership to my class and the entire fitness club and never came back. She broke my heart.

Though sad that she did not love my Jesus, I felt personally persecuted. The Word tells us everyone who lives a godly life in Christ Jesus will suffer persecution, which gives us cause to rejoice. I should have been rejoicing. My error was that I let a flaming dart of hurt get past my shield of faith, or maybe I had laid that shield aside. I felt my health exit my body as the enemy gladly stepped in. Halt, halt, halt! Now I had no choice.

Indeed, I loved Jesus, and certainly, He had called me according to His purpose. "But why Lord, why such a harsh discipline? How can I help people in my present state? What will happen to my classes, my students?" See the undertone here? I was all concerned about my stuff, my efforts, and my control of them.

Turning inwardly, I tried to figure it all out, which is always the wrong thing to do. Such a maze in my thinking followed. I was leaning to my own understanding! That gave Satan a toehold in my body, soul, and spirit. I could not see that it was because I failed to stand and to halt when my loving Lord said to do these two things. He had been warning me in order to protect me.

While I do not like to talk about the strange things that happened to me, I will do so because it may help you better understand the wiles of the devil and the power of Jesus the Christ.

Think about it:

When we hear the instructive voice of the Lord, and we do not obey it, there will be consequences.

Leaning, Leaning, but on What?

> Trust in the Lord with all of your heart and lean not to your own understanding. In all your ways acknowledge Him and He shall direct your paths.
> (Proverbs 3:5–6, NKJV).

Read that again, please.

Strange and seemingly unrelated symptoms plagued me for a long time. My doctor told me there was nothing more she could do because none of the tests she administered showed anything wrong with me. She refused to see me anymore for the same symptoms, although nothing she had come up with had helped me in the least. She concluded that it must be stress.

I experienced dizziness, allergy symptoms, itching all over, tunnel vision, rapid heart rate, and low blood pressure, not to mention debilitating fatigue, body aches, and fever. My hair was falling out, and all of my fingernails broke off and stopped growing. The results of every physical test I took came back normal. I saw an optometrist, an endocrinologist, a neuro-ophthalmologist, a cardiologist, and an ear, nose, and throat doctor. Each took me through a plethora of tests and exercises, all yielding the same results. Two MRIs and a CAT scan revealed nothing abnormal. It would appear that I was the most normal person on planet earth. The doctors were baffled as they searched for a label to attach to the strange things happening to me.

At the same time, I was in my head a lot, continuing to be intensely grieved at how other people were or were not doing things. I felt precious energy going out of me and into this whole situation. Of course, I brought these things before the Lord in prayer, but deep down, I was hanging onto them with a tight grip. My despair was because these other people operated at what I believed was below standard. As if I could change them by worrying. Such a waste of time, emotion, and energy! I was clearly out of bounds in my thinking.

Doubt entered my mind. I began to question myself and to deny my calling. Maybe I should get a stay-at-home internet job. An okay thing? Of course, but not for me, because it was outside of the place where God had called me: to dance, whether dancing myself, choreographing, teaching it, teaching about it, or writing about it.

He always returned me and refreshed me through dance, just as He will refresh you through your particular calling. Furthermore, He had given me an assignment, and I was trying to get out of it. That's what illness and fatigue were doing to me. The enemy was trying to take me out.

Take a moment to assess yourself and ask God to search your heart for any control issues you may be trying to hold. Ask Him also to show you if any doubt is creeping in. Then get into His Word and be encouraged that He is for you, not against you. Get it into your head and on your lips that He is your Healer.

I prayed every day, "Lord, I am Yours. Show me what You want. Where do You want me?" He is faithful to hear and answer our prayers. However, I could not hear His answers. He seemed far away from me. I did not feel His presence like I was used to. But who moved? As I leaned more and more to my own understanding, He let me flounder and flop. As I looked outside His call for me, He lovingly taught me that He really does know best.

My quest for answers continued. In lacking something I think I need, I am forced to rely on God.

Notes from my pastor

- "In a storm, STAND, pray for light, do not seek a way out, stand!" Humm, where had I heard that before? But on I went, seeking a way out, not only out of the problem, but out of my calling. Indeed, this was profoundly serious.
- "The more territory the enemy is allowed, the more the truth will be persecuted." Though true in a larger sense, this gem applied to me, too. As I looked away from the Lord to find the answers I desperately wanted, the enemy was happy to provide plenty of them.
- "Faith works only in the now and brings substantial evidence."

    "Now faith is the substance of things hoped for, the evidence of things not seen" (Hebrews 11:1, NKJV).

    I think it works on the flip side too. I had substantial evidence of my lack of

faith. Truly it was all manifesting in my
body, soul, and spirit.

- "Confess the answer, not the problem." I knew this.
  I tried to do this. Yet, I kept telling people about
  my physical issues. In so doing I was canceling my
  prayers and creating more issues.

  "Death and life are in the power of
  the tongue, and those who love it will eat
  its fruit" (Proverbs 18:21, NKJV)

- "Look above your circumstances, into the eyes of
  Jesus." This is key. We must look at Him and stop
  looking at, analyzing, and talking about what is
  wrong.
- "Corrupt speech is saying that you are sick when
  the Word says you are healed."

  "Lord, I love You. Lord, I want to
  serve You. Lord, I believe Your Word." I
  can honestly say I wanted only to please
  Him. He promised healing as a part of
  salvation. I believed it. "By His Stripes I
  was Healed!" (1 Peter 2:24).

For many years, my prayer had been that I would walk
in divine health. I wanted Him to be proud of me. He already
told me, "no good thing dwells in my flesh." My desire to lift
myself in the flesh is always a sin. It is pride, and it is what
caused Satan to fall. Thinking it is me is one of his subtle
ways to trip us up. It's so human. Yet, thinking this way is

soulish because it exalts self above God. It is the "me god" again, and it is an idol we must tear down.

While my desire to walk in divine health was correct, my attitude about it was not. That desire must have as its purpose the glorifying of God. As He is lifted, He will draw all people to Himself.

> No one has ascended to heaven but He who came down from heaven, that is, the Son of Man who is in heaven. And as Moses lifted up the serpent (symbolic of all sin) in the wilderness, even so must the Son of Man be lifted up, that whoever believes in Him should not perish but have eternal life.
>
> John 3:13–15 (NKJV)

I was getting it, finally. I do the lifting; He does the saving. Beneath the surface, God was working. He showed me a vision. Words can't adequately describe it, but hopefully, you will get the idea. I saw myself as a little human being, and then, above me, I saw the expanse of the glory of God. I knew everything we ever need or desire resides in His glory. Philippians 4:19 (NKJV) says: "And my God shall supply all your need according to His riches in glory by Christ Jesus." I then saw myself reaching into His glory and pulling out health and stability for myself. If everything we need is found within His glory, how do we access it? Certainly, we have to be clean before Him and we must reach into it in faith that we do receive those things for which we have asked.

On the one hand, there is me in the natural realm. On the other hand, there is the glory of God, a higher reality. It is by asking, seeking, and knocking that we can bring the glory of God over into our natural realm. Within the glory of God is everything we could need or desire.

But why was I still sick? Back and forth, up and down, it flowed. Sometimes I felt like working, sometimes not, and sometimes I went to church, sometimes not. Going upstairs to the bathroom wore me out. I counted it as a day of accomplishment if I washed the dishes or did the laundry.

The following is from my journal. I was slipping:

What it is, it is. (I hate that expression.) I still don't know why I am sick or what to do about it. If this is what Jesus wants, then so be it.

Error! In looking at the situation rather than looking to Jesus, I began to accept the illness as my own. Did I forget the stripes Jesus took on His back by which I was healed?

Continuing from my journal:

I have told Him that I am His.
I do not care for my life.
I just want Him to be glorified in me.
For some reason that is not happening.
I believe the Word.
I believe in healing.
Yet it is not for me.
I can't even say the right things in conversations with others, although it is not that I am even trying to say anything. Why? I simply want to be able to contribute to those both inside and outside of my sphere of influence and take a step forward, towards healing.
Forget it. I don't care.

Well, of course, I cared. This monologue was born of frustration and fatigue. More questions arose in my mind. Was this a test? Was He burning away everything in my heart that wasn't right? My days consisted of sitting around being dizzy, forcing myself to do a few things around the house. I took a leave of absence from all work activities, including even thinking about work. I wondered if I was dying. I thought a lot about eternity, and I began to see myself in light of it.

My journal entries changed a little:

Praise the Lord, the Maker of heaven and earth!
I was made to praise You, Lord! But how can I do that in my present state? What more do I need to do? Have I been

enough of a blessing to others? Have I represented Your Kingdom well? Any final instructions?

Heaven and earth are full of Your Glory, Lord. Thank You, Jesus for forgiving all my sin and healing all of my diseases.

I feel so removed from this earthly life. No more whining about why.

I am Yours, Lord. Do with me as You will. I want to see You and hear You more clearly.

Are we done?"

He answered, "NOT YET!"

I was disappointed! So desperately wanting it to be over, I spiraled swiftly downward. As I sunk into the gray world of depression, I had no passion for anything, no creativity, indeed, nothing to say about anything. I turned inward. I wondered if my life been my own pursuit with a Christian veneer? Had it been to prove myself? Had I lost my life to find it, or had it merely resurfaced with so-called goodness? Doubt filled my soul. "Did God really say this?" The enemy was trying to paralyze me like a bug caught in a spider web. Without the love and the care of the Lord, I would have died there! Only Jesus could free me from this!

Think about it:

In lacking something that I think I need, I am forced to rely on God.

Wafting in the Wind

> If any of you lacks wisdom, let him ask of God, who gives to all liberally and without reproach, and it will be given to him. But let him ask in faith, with no doubting, for he who doubts is like a wave of the sea driven and tossed by the wind. For let not that man suppose that he will receive anything from the Lord; he is a double-minded man, unstable in all his ways.
>
> James 1:5–8 (NKJV)

"Ok, I am asking: why, Lord?" I was overworked and tired, but I kept pushing onward. I believe this created a breach in the spirit that allowed two little darts to pierce my soul. The first was when I was ghosted, and I took it into my heart and allowed it to wound me greviously. The second was when I let my client's rebuke of Biblical wisdom hurt me personally. In this weakened condition, I heard the voice of the Lord but did not obey it. Stand and halt were pretty clear words He spoke to me. I was a hearer only, not a doer of His (Rhema) word.

Hearing and not doing causes confusion in our minds and hearts. I began to be more and more dissatisfied with everyone and everything around me. In this totally dissatisfied condition, which was full of confusion, I began to doubt that God wanted to heal me. This doubt was paralyzing. I couldn't think or see straight.

Only Jesus could free me from this maze of thought. As I sat in my chair daily, I read, I prayed, "Where is this breakthrough I am supposed to have? Where is Your healing, Lord?" I believed He would heal me, and I confessed it, sometimes. My attitude was that I was waiting on God to heal me. Be sure this is not what you are doing. Such an attitude demonstrates a lack of faith. But remember the note from my pastor: "Faith works only in the now and brings *substantial evidence.*"

Faith works in the present tense, not in the past and not in the future. I knew I was supposed to be learning something in this, but what was it? Jesus intervened here. Had He not, I think I would have died. He gave me a little remission. I felt much better and enjoyed a flurry of housework for about three days, but by day four, I was back in my chair again.

There was a major conflict in my heart. I remember one day, actually one of many, when I woke up ready to go to work, absolutely looking forward to it. A few minutes later, I did not want to go at all, and I had no energy to do so. I found myself praying that no one would show up to take my class. Wow! I was that deep in doubt, defeat, and depression. I felt the same about church, the same with everything. I searched myself: was I disobedient? How could I glorify God like this? Why this conflict?

"Lord, help me. I need wisdom!"

"How can I bless You from my chair?"

"How am I blessing the people You have placed in my life?"

Desperately pleading with the Lord seemed to avail nothing. So I concluded that it was time to act. This reaction was wrong: I was leaning to my own understanding, again. So began the Doctor Era. Six months into the unnamed illness, I began a quest. I searched the medical community for answers. My primary care physician said I was normal in every way, though I certainly did not feel normal. She ordered a CAT scan and an MRI, but neither revealed anything out of the ordinary. My eye doctor ordered a second MRI to ensure nothing could be causing my eye problems. Although my vision was blurred and getting worse, the tests showed no reason for those symptoms. My doctor friend said it might be low cortisol. I studied about that and ordered supplements to address the issue. No change.

I saw a neuro-ophthalmologist for issues related to dizziness. He ordered a vestibular system test and a tilt test, and the latter was a real trip! I was strapped to a table, which then tilted me into an upright position where I had to stand for 45 minutes to monitor how my heart rate would be affected. It was stable, albeit a bit high. Continuing my quest, I visited a neurologist next. After several questions and an exam, he concluded that I had no neurological disorders.

Next stop: a cardiologist diagnosed me with POTS, a diagnosis which I firmly reject. Postural orthostatic tachycardia syndrome, or POTS, greatly simplified, is a condition where one's heart rate is too high and blood pressure too low. While there were other symptoms to confirm this diagnosis, I knew in my heart, and still know, that these particular manifestations were a direct result of the stress in my body, mind, and spirit. He prescribed me two medications. Both of them had known side effects that were the same as the symptoms I was experiencing, precisely the opposite of what I needed. Fed up with conventional medicine, I visited a nurse practitioner who specialized in natural, holistic healing. She further tested me and gave me advice that, while helpful, ultimately caused no change in my condition. By this time, I was angry. I got a glimpse of how evil my human heart is in turning from God: not trusting Him and being mad at my situation. Our sinful nature is so strong. Only the Holy Spirit can tame it.

Another short remission followed this quest, but soon after, I plunged into the valley of death again. My big problem: I was still talking sickness, not healing, most of the time. God brought this lesson home to me during my healing. If you learn nothing else from reading about what I went through, remember this, "Death and life are in the power of the tongue, and those who love it will eat its fruit" (Proverbs 18:21, NKJV). Learn to speak life! When we pray for healing and then confess sickness, we have just canceled our prayer. And remember this nugget from my pastor, "Corrupt speech is saying that you are sick when the Word says you are healed."

Every test result came back normal.

Additionally, during this Doctor Era, there had been a shift in the management at the fitness club where I worked. I was now required to chase prospective members down and get them to buy a membership. This grieved my heart. My body did not do well with the stress of sales on top of everything else. Mercifully, God directed me to an online webinar about sales. The moderator said this, which was a great relief to me: "Never call a prospect more than twice. More than twice is chasing them. No need to chase anyone. You have better things to do." You know, God will bring us the people to us that we need to achieve His purposes. I have seen this so many times. Have you?

I sincerely wanted to work, but my body wasn't cooperating. I was out of sync body, soul, and spirit. Nevertheless, I went to work when I could, but it was not fun. I felt hopeless. But God! He is the bringer of hope!

Enter Job's friends! Like his friends, my friends had plenty of advice.

I got lots of advice from my friends!

One told me to stop all supplements for a couple of weeks. I did stop them, but I felt no different. Another said, "No, it sounds like gluten intolerance." I stopped eating gluten for three weeks. No change. Yet another told me to stop all dairy, and products containing dairy, because they must be causing my congestion. This trial availed nothing either. Then came the friend who said I should eat only whole organic foods and cut out processed foods. Though this is great advice and something everyone should do, I felt no relief at this juncture. And then there were the ones who said to add this supplement, add that food, etc. Nothing made one tiny little bit of difference.

As a fitness expert, I strongly believe in proper diet and exercise, but this was not my particular problem at this time. My level of desperation was growing deeper and darker. I knew something was seriously wrong when, at a prayer meeting, I was blank: I heard nothing, thought nothing, had nothing to say. Being this way was a place where I had never been before, and it was frightening.

Though I spoke the Word over myself, I did not yet believe it. I honored Him when I spoke in agreement with His Word, but then I confessed sickness. That was being double-minded and, therefore, unstable in all my ways. Where was my heart? More problems developed. I experienced muscle aches and digestive issues. On it went. The cycle continued and repeated itself many times: sick, better, sick again. Over and over, this pattern continued, for more than two years.

God is always faithful, and through all of this, He was teaching me many things about myself. Here is an interesting key He gave me. Truthfully, I had never thought about this before. All my life, I have looked to some person to encourage me and cheer me on. When that person fainted or left, I faltered. Jesus wants to be the One, yet I was faltering without that human to lean on. Why? Do I not trust Him? Believe Him? As a teen, it was my dance teachers. When I went out on my own, there was no one, so I missed a beat or two. Then it was teachers again, and friends, and after that, my wonderful mother-in-law. Then there was no one, and I faltered for a long time.

I continued to look for admiration and affirmation from people, especially men, and invariably they failed me. That's what people do. Only Jesus can meet the need I had been trying to fill with humans. Gratefully, I did later learn this lesson. Please check yourself on this too. Is there some person you depend on for affirmation before you receive it from God? Is that a *person god* or idol?

Time for a deeper and more fundamental heart check:

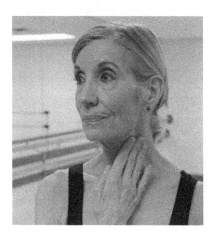

Check your heart.

Are you looking to anyone or anything other than Jesus to fill your deepest needs? He loves you so much, and you can trust Him. He will never, ever leave you. It is like this, every person who ever lived has turned from God and attempted to do it his or her own way: *every* person.

That is what He calls sin: going our own way without Him. So, here is what you must do, if you haven't done so already. Tell Him you are sorry for living without Him and admit you are a sinner: you have gone your own way and not depended on Him. Ask Him to forgive You and to give you a new heart to serve Him. Use your own words and pour out your heart to Him. Tell Him you accept His payment for your sins: His sacrificial blood shed on the cross. Ask Him to forgive you and heal you physically, mentally, and spiritually, and give you an eternity with Him. He will do it. But don't stop there! Ask Jesus to baptize you in His Holy Spirit. He is your power to be His witness. Read the Bible so you can learn about these things. Seek out a church family who loves Jesus and where you can learn His Word.

Back to my story. I took a second leave of absence from work, and I rested with Jesus this time. Having no job pressure, no students, no real responsibilities was wonderful for a season. The Lord woke me up every day at 5:00 a.m. to study the Bible and pray. It is a habit I have kept until this day. That time was, and is, the highlight of my day. He took me through a measure of healing, and He took any of my burdens as I would give them to Him. But we weren't quite there yet. My symptoms continued to ebb and flow.

Because He loves us, when we don't heed His still, small voice, He amplifies it. During this episode of rest, I began to hear Him again. My mind was cluttered with what I thought He wanted, but His voice was more discernible when my head was less jumbled. The Holy Spirit is often quelled when we do what we think He wants and are so busy carrying out those things that we are not hearing Him. The tools He has placed in our hands are to be picked up and used as He directs. But, when we run ahead of Him and start doing our own thing, those tools can become obstacles to hearing His voice. It is the "me god" again, ever so stealthy pulling at us.

Formulas quell the Holy Spirit. We must come to Him open to hear what He wants, not proceed with our program, and ask Him to bless it. I don't know how to implement this or how it will play out even as I write this. I yield myself to His desires. How many times do I have to lay it down? As many as it takes. It is an ongoing, lifelong process. As the Apostle Paul said, "I die daily" (1 Corinthians 15:31, NKJV).

I had to lay down the things that were making me sick. To repeat, these things initially were:

- Overworking and stressing about it.
- Not giving the Lord the proper credit and acknowledgment because of what people would think.
- Wanting others to push ahead at my pace, in my way.
- Being deeply grieved with issues at work or in others that were not perfect in my mind and those who were not pushing ahead of where I thought they should be.
- Resenting because of the belief that I was not allowed to use my gifts at work.

These led to not obeying His voice, confusion, dissatisfaction, doubt, and depression.

I was confused, dissatisfied, doubting, and depressed.

Think about it:

You can trust Jesus! He will never, ever leave you!

Forage if You Must

> Do not be wise in your own eyes;
> fear the LORD and depart from evil. It
> will be health to your flesh, and strength
> to your bones (Proverbs 3:7–8, NKJV).

My pet bird knows all about foraging. My husband and I like to put his favorite treat, cashews, at the bottom of his food dish. We cover them with good but less preferred snacks. He puts his little beak into the dish and throws out the things on top. Then he digs for that cashew. This is a good example of how we need to forage for truth.

He foraged and found his favorite treat, the cashew.

Pontius Pilate said, "What is truth?" (John 18:38) People today talk about *your* truth and *my* truth. Truth is not relative; it is absolute. It never changes, no matter what people think. We cannot turn away from Jesus, who is *the* Truth, to serve self, despite the popular way of thinking. To do so is to put self in the place reserved for God, thus making self an idol. People have done this throughout history. It's the "me god" again! Let's trust and obey Jesus, Who is *the* Truth.

In reading Deuteronomy, I am impressed with how thoroughly the Lord addresses this. Although written to Israel, it applies to you and me. If we are believers in Jesus, born of His Spirit, then we are grafted into Israel. Though no longer under the curse of the law, its principles still apply to us. The Israelites' slavery in Egypt is a picture of our slavery in the world, with its idolatrous ways, before accepting His gift of salvation.

> I make this covenant and this oath, not with you alone, but with him who stands here with us today before the LORD our God, as well as with him who is not here with us today (for you know that we dwelt in the land of Egypt and that we came through the nations which you passed by, and you saw their abominations and their idols which were among them—wood and stone and silver and gold); so that there may not be among you man or woman or family or tribe, whose heart turns away from the LORD our God, to go and serve the gods of these nations, and that there may not be among you a root bearing bitterness or

> wormwood; and so it may not happen,
> when he hears the words of this curse,
> that he blesses himself in his heart, say-
> ing, 'I shall have peace, even though I fol-
> low the dictates of my heart'—as though
> the drunkard could be included with the
> sober.
> Deuteronomy 29:14–19 (NKJV)

Our heart will always deceive us if it is not subject to the Lord of all. It desperately wants to be the "me god," and it will lead us astray. Do not forget this. Life is not about pleasing others. It is about Truth.

> Jesus said to him, 'I am the way, the
> truth, and the life. No one comes to the
> Father except through Me' (John 14:6,
> NKJV).

In this world of "truths," how can we know what is and is not *The Truth*? It is simple yet challenging. The only way we can understand what is and what is not truth is by filtering our thoughts and beliefs through the Word of God. If something doesn't line up with the Bible, we have to discard it. That won't make sense to the world. They will hate us for it. They hate us because the Word exposes their sinful condition and their need for Him. Before my salvation, I thought Christians were always blaming me for my lifestyle. Only after receiving Jesus did I realize that phenomenon as conviction from the Holy Spirit. Have you had this experience?

After I tried to solve my illness by leaning to my own understanding, I diligently sought the Lord and His wisdom. Too bad I did not do this first, right? There was just more

He wanted me to face. I allowed Him to turn His searchlight into my heart. He showed me some worldly mindsets that had rooted themselves into my thoughts and ways. These things had to go.

- I had to renounce my bondage to gaining wealth by the power of my hand, how well I perform my calling, my job. It is something I must continually do.

> You say in your heart, "My power and the might of my hand have gained me this wealth. And you shall remember the Lord your God, for it is He who gives you power to get wealth that He may establish His covenant which He swore to your fathers, as it is this day."
> Deuteronomy 8:17–18 (NKJV)

- I remembered from where I had fallen, I repented and began to do the things I did when I first met Jesus. I told everyone about Him. He was my first thought in the morning, my last in the evening

> Nevertheless, I have this against you, that you have left your first love. Remember therefore from where you have fallen; repent and do the first works, or else I will come to you quickly and remove your lampstand from its place—unless you repent.
> Revelation 2:4–5 (NKJV)

I renewed my commitment to guard my mouth. "Whoever guards his mouth and tongue keeps **his** soul from troubles" (Proverbs 21:23, NKJV).

I reminded myself that I am His ambassador. I am to represent His kingdom on this earth. "Now then, we are ambassadors for Christ, as though God were pleading through us: we implore you on Christ's behalf, be reconciled to God" (2 Corinthians 5:20, NKJV).

• I determined to serve Him alone, not depending on anyone else.

How many people stood up for the Lord in Daniel's day? Three. How many people kept openly praying when it was declared unlawful? One. Daniel loved the Lord and obeyed Him. He was a beloved leader, yet he was alone. The Lord revealed secrets to him and preserved his life against naturally impossible odds. Let's revisit the vision that the Lord showed me earlier. I had filed it in memory when He gave it to me, but He brought it to mind again. I saw myself as a little human, and then, to my right and above me, I saw the expanse of the glory of God. I knew that everything we ever need or desire resides in His glory. Philippians 4:19 (NKJV) says, "And my God shall supply all your need according to His riches in glory by Christ Jesus."

I then saw myself reaching into His glory and pulling out health and stability for myself. If everything we need is found within His glory, how do we access it? Indeed, we have to be clean before Him, and we must reach into it in faith that we do receive those things for which we have asked.

To further explain what I saw: On the one hand, there is me in the natural realm. On the other hand, there is the glory of God, a higher reality. It is by asking, seeking, and knocking that we can bring the glory of God over into our natural realm. Within the glory of God is everything we could need or desire.

The spiritual realm is very real but is a totally different realm than the one we see with our eyes. It is by obedience to His Word and communion with Him that we can pull His glory, with all of its benefits and blessings, into our natural lives. "While we do not look at the things which are seen, but at the things which are not seen. For the things which are seen are temporary, but the things which are not seen are eternal" (2 Corinthians 4:18, NKJV).

We as humans tend to respond to what we can perceive physically. But, once born again and filled with His Spirit, we can choose to walk in the spiritual realm. The Word tells us to "Walk in the Spirit and you shall not fulfill the lust of the flesh" (Galatians 5:16, NKJV).

We are a spirit, we have a soul, and we live in a body. God is a Spirit, and we are to worship Him in spirit and in truth. To worship in spirit is to worship from your heart. To worship in truth is to worship from your current situation in life. When the Lord says He is seeking worshippers to worship Him in spirit and in truth, He means He is seeking those who will worship Him from their heart, not their head: right where they are at any given moment in time. Yes, you can worship Him out of a broken heart or out of pain and suffering. To do so transfers the burden to Him, which is where it needs to be.

Think about it:

The *only* way we can know what is truth is by filtering our thoughts and beliefs through the Word of God.

Be Healed. Finally!

> Bless the Lord, O my soul; And all
> that is within me, bless His holy name!
> Bless the LORD, O my soul, And forget
> not all His benefits: Who forgives all your
> iniquities, Who heals all your diseases,
> Who redeems your life from destruction,
> Who crowns you with lovingkindness
> and tender mercies, Who satisfies your
> mouth with good things, So that your
> youth is renewed like the eagle's.
>
> Psalm 103:1–5 (NKJV)

These are promises from God to us. I think it is plain that
He wants us, His children, to enjoy His absolute best in every
area of life. As time progressed and my illnesses' ups and
downs continued, I was exhausted and sick of feeling bad
and missing things because I was too ill to participate. I had
pretty much resolved that I would always be like that because
I had been in it for over two years. I was looking in the wrong
place for healing. I was looking in the natural realm and not
the spiritual realm.

One Sunday, during the praise and worship segment
at church, the congregation was singing, and I was praying,
"Lord, please heal my allergy symptoms, my dizziness, and
my itching. Please, Lord restore my energy and take away

my aches and pains. Help me be able to maintain a train of thought and be able to speak again. PLEASE, Lord!"

It was on this rather normal Sunday morning that Jesus spoke to me very clearly behind my left shoulder and said, "Drop it!"

"Drop it!"

"I know about all of these things, I have heard this so much, I've got it. Drop it!"

This time I did not question or stumble at His rhema word to me. I really did it this time. I answered Him: "Okay, Lord, I will. I am not going to think about it, I am not going to talk about it, I am not going to pray about it anymore. I am going to drop it! It's Yours!"

Immediately this scripture came to mind: "Cast all your anxiety on him because He cares for you" (1 Peter 5:7).

From that moment, the symptoms started to disappear. One at a time, I felt them leave my body. First, the allergy symptoms and then the itching left, followed by the aches and pains. By the afternoon, my eyes were in focus, and I was no longer dizzy. The remaining aggravations dissipated out of my body within 24 hours. My normal energy returned by the next morning. Hallelujah! Yes, this really happened! It was truly a miracle! "Thank You, Lord! I will tell everyone this story of your miraculous healing in me!"

Now realize that it is important that you can't just suddenly say "drop it" and be healed: should God want to do it that way, He certainly can because He is God. But it is not a formula. In the previous chapters, I have taken you on a journey through my healing process. Yours will, no doubt, be different. But I want to be sure that nothing that was hindering me is hindering you. Got it?

Here is a summary of all the things the Lord lovingly brought me through.

1. Overworking, stressing about everything beyond my control, and allowing myself to be wounded by a friend who left and a client who complained all combined in me to result in this strange illness with no name. All of these things did not occur overnight, but they had been building over time.
2. Most importantly, I heard the Lord tell me to stand and then to halt, but I did not obey Him, partly because I didn't know how to do these things, but possibly because I didn't want to do them.
3. My focus was always on myself, not on Him. In my totally dissatisfied condition, which was full of confusion, I began to doubt that God wanted me to be healed.

4. It decided it was time to act. Six months into the unnamed illness, I began a quest. Although this could be okay for you, for me, it signified leaning to my own understanding. This was not a thing for the doctors to uncover in my case.

5. All of my friends, like Job's friends, told me what my problem was. None of them had anything that could help me.

6. I had to renounce my bondage to gaining wealth by the power of my hand and how well I perform my calling, my job. This is something we must continually do.

7. I remembered from where I had fallen, I repented, and I began to do the things I did when I first met Jesus.

8. I renewed my commitment to guard my mouth.

9. I reminded myself that I am His ambassador. I am to represent His Kingdom on this earth faithfully.

10. I determined to serve Him alone, not depending on anyone else.

Again, your journey is different in the incidentals, but are the basics not basically the same? Search your heart, get right, and be healed today! Let everything go that is not of Him. When the Lord had fully taught me all of these things, and I had made changes in my soul and spirit, I was ready to receive His healing. If we boil it all down to the absolute bottom line, all of my issues and blockages to being well were because I put myself and my knowledge above trusting God completely. He had to reveal this to me because I was unaware of it at the time. Again, Proverbs 3:5, "Trust in the Lord with all your heart and lean not to your own understanding."

When the Lord told me to "drop it" and I obeyed I noticed that my conversation changed. I no longer referred to *my* symptoms, but rather *the* symptoms. They were not mine anymore; I left them with Jesus. My pastor looked at "drop it" from a different perspective: He said it could be that the Lord told the angels to drop healing on me. While everything God says is multi-faceted, I believe that I was the one who needed to do the dropping.

During this two-and-one-half-year episode, the Lord gave me a song. It's not a new or original song, but it is one that He definitely put in my heart and even in my mouth. Often, I found myself humming it. I would even wake up humming it. Written in the eighth century, originally in Gaelic, it is one of the oldest, if not the oldest hymns that we still have today, "Be Thou My Vision." What a love for Jesus the author had! It is my love song to Him too. As you read the lyrics below, let them permeate your soul and spirit.

> Be thou my vision, O Lord of my heart
> Naught be all else to me, save that thou art
> Thou my best thought, by day or by night
> Waking or sleeping, thy presence my light
> Be thou my wisdom, and thou my true word
> I ever with thee and thou with me, Lord
> Thou my great Father, and I thy true son
> Thou in me dwelling and I with thee one
> Riches I heed not, nor vain, empty praise
> Thou mine inheritance, now and always
> Thou and thou only first in my heart
> High King of heaven, my treasure thou art
> High King of heaven, my victory won
> May I reach heaven's joys, O bright heaven's sun
> Heart of my own heart, whatever befall

Still be my vision, O ruler of all
Heart of my own heart, whatever befall
Still be my vision, O ruler of all.

What about you? Although this is the story of my healing, this book is for you. Certainly, the Lord has been at your side during your reading, whatever your relationship with Him. Allow Him to search your heart. Write down what He shows you. Ask Him to show it to you in a song, a scripture, or through someone else. Listen. Learn. Obey.

Now on the other side of this story, I can see in retrospect how He loved me and taught me the whole way through it. My relationship with Him has deepened, and I am more passionate about telling of His great love as I share this story. Before, I believed in my head what Isaiah 53:5 says, "By His stripes we [were] healed." Now it is a deep conviction within me that He truly did heal me when He took the stripes on His back. I know that, in Him, healing is mine. I am to walk in health at all times. The afflictions that come against us are from the world, the flesh, or the devil. They are to be rebuked and rejected by the authority Jesus gave us. Hallelujah, what a Savior! I pray that the many things I had to learn and the lessons from the Lord will bless you, strengthen you and build a rock-solid faith in you that God wants you to be well.

Think about it:

We must never own an illness, indeed, any attack from the enemy of our souls!

Lessons from God's Heart

May you be blessed by the following nuggets of wisdom from His heart.

Words

Immediately after my healing, I started saying *the* symptoms, not *my* symptoms. For me, this was a radical shift toward Biblical thinking, a perspective Jesus wants all of us to have. The victory is always His. I will never, ever, again say *my* illness or *my* symptoms! Whatever the reason for them, I will never again claim them as my own. The first of the lessons I learned: We must never own an illness, indeed, any attack from the enemy of our souls! To do so only reinforces them in body, mind, and spirit.

The Word teaches that "death and life are in the power of the tongue: and they that love it shall eat the fruit thereof" (Proverbs 18:21, KJV). That means we can talk death, or we can talk life. Whichever one we choose will result in its fulfillment. To say *my* sickness, *my* issue, **my** whatever, takes it out of God's hands. We must learn to speak life, not death. This is a hard habit to break, but we must break it if we are to live a victorious life. We must learn what the Word says about us and confess those things and apply them personally. For example:

- "By His stripes I was healed" (1 Peter 2:24).

- "He sent His Word and healed my disease" (Psalm 107:20).
- "I am prospering and in health, as my soul prospers" (3 John 1:2).
- "He forgives all my sin and heals all my diseases" (Psalm 103:3).

It is a great idea to write out your own confessions based on the Word and confess them over yourself regularly. There is a section in the workbook chapter of this book for you to record them. Look at the following Scriptures for starters: "Beloved, I pray that all may go well with you and that you may be in good health, even as your soul is well" (3 John 1:2, NKJV).

> Surely he has borne our grief and carried our sorrows; Yet we esteemed him stricken, smitten of God, and afflicted. But he was wounded for our transgressions, he was bruised for our iniquities; the chastisement of our peace was upon him, and by his stripes we are healed.
>
> Isaiah 53:4–5 (NKJV)

> When He was in a certain city, a man full of leprosy, upon seeing Jesus, fell on his face and begged Him, 'Lord, if You will, You can make me clean.' He reached out His hand and touched him, saying, 'I will. Be clean.' And immediately the leprosy left him.
>
> Luke 5:12–13 (NKJV)

Our words frame our world. Bad confessions work as well as good ones.

I know someone who says things like:

- "My kids are always sick."
- "My wife is always tired."
- "Work is always a pain."
- "My body hurts."
- "I'm sick."

Can you imagine how their life is?

- Their kids are always sick.
- Their wife is always tired.
- Their job is always a pain.
- Their body hurts.
- They are sick.

What if they would rather choose life and speak the opposite things into their life?

- "My kids are healthy."
- "My wife's strength is renewed."
- "Work is a place where I can help and be an influence for good."
- "My body is healed by the stripes that Jesus bore a very long time ago."
- "I am prospering and in health as my soul prospers."

If they spoke life in this manner, what would their life be like? You know the answer to that, don't you?

Do you want to be healed?

Although this was not my issue, it is, nevertheless, something else to consider. Do you want to be healed?

> Now there is in Jerusalem near the Sheep Gate a pool, which in Aramaic is called Bethesda and which is surrounded by five covered colonnades. Here a great number of disabled people used to lie— the blind, the lame, the paralyzed.
>
> John 5:2–3

There were many sick people there. One version says "a great multitude" (John 5:3, NKJV). They were all lying around on their mats, waiting for an angel to come and stir the waters so that if they were in the right place at the right time, they might be healed. Jesus goes on to tell of a man who had been there for thirty-eight years! Jesus saw him lying there on his mat and asked him, "Do you want to get well?" (John 5:6). Check this out: He answered, "I have no one to help me into the pool when the water is stirred. While I am trying to get in, someone else goes down ahead of me" (John 5:7).

Why didn't the sick guy just say, "Yes?" I think he didn't want to be healed right then because he did not want the responsibility that would come with it. It is easier to be affirmed, established, and pitied rather than to change. However, Jesus calls us to change. The man on the mat had been there for so long that it had become his identity. He had other friends on mats, and they would talk about their issues together. They had developed a culture. Had he been healed, he would have to give up his identity and change his way of life. What about us? Could it be that some of us have had an issue for so long that we really don't want to be healed? We want Jesus to love us and comfort us in our affliction. Additionally, the man said no one would help him. Do we blame our issues on someone else who didn't help us, affirm us, and enable us?

Today brokenness has become an idol, and people defend their right to bow down to it. They want to be like the man on the mat, gathering with others with like symptoms and talking about their afflictions, thus magnifying and further establishing them. They, too, have a culture. It is the voice of enablement, and to be healed, we have to break it.

"Then Jesus said to him, 'Get up! Pick up your mat and walk'" (John 5:8). He told the sick guy to do something he previously could not do: to get up and walk. He will do the same for us if we will get off the mat of our issues and walk.

Lord, help us to get off of our mats and be healed. Grant us the boldness to get up and walk. You are God of the impossible. We believe this! In Jesus' Name, amen.

Noise

Could noise be a factor that causes stress for you? I wrote this piece on this subject: Sleep passes me by as random thoughts fill my mind. Meaningless data streams compete for my attention. They are noise to me, like static on the phone when I try to have a conversation with a friend.

I sense that perhaps I am too involved with my life's little ups and downs and how everything affects me. But, my life is not really mine anymore. I gave it to Jesus some years back. Now, I am here to accomplish His will in the time and space He has given to me. Still, the noise continues in my brain, but it is growing weaker as I think of Jesus and how much He loves me.

- What will people think if I wear that red shirt? Noise.
- Will I have enough strength to do all the things I need to do today? Noise.
- What will I have for lunch? Noise.
- Will Mary be there to help me with the new project? Noise.
- Will they ever take care of the things in the building that need attention? Noise.

What is my life? It is a vapor.

> Whereas you do not know what will happen tomorrow. For what *is* your life? It is even a vapor that appears for a little time and then vanishes away (James 4:14, NKJV).

Remembering that, my perspective rights itself. I begin to praise Him:

> Bless the Lord, O my soul; And all that is within me, bless His holy name! Bless the LORD, O my soul, And forget not all His benefits: Who forgives all your iniquities, Who heals all your diseases, Who redeems your life from destruction, Who crowns you with lovingkindness and tender mercies, Who satisfies your

mouth with good things, So that your
youth is renewed like the eagle's.

Psalm 103:1–5 (NKJV)

The next sound I hear is the alarm clock rousing me
six hours later from sweet sleep. I had found the cure for the
noise.

Sleep or lack of sleep

Having been a professional ballet dancer, instructor,
personal trainer, etc., my whole life, my body has suffered
some abuse. In my late 60s, I continue to teach barre and
ballet classes demonstrating everything full out because I love
it. Lately, my doctor says I have worn out my lumbar spine. I
certainly won't let that stop me! The Lord is teaching me how
to avoid pain there when I am teaching.

When I come home after teaching three classes in a row,
it is a different story. My whole body aches. I do Epsom salt
baths, heating pad, ice, you name it, but what really does it
for me is sleep. When I say sleep, I don't mean a 15-minute
nap or even a 3-hour nap. I am talking about 8–10 hours of
deep, restorative sleep.

Working out physically tears down our muscles. It is
during times of rest that they are repairing and building.
When we enjoy that long deep sleep, not only are our muscles rebuilding, but our entire body is healing. May this be
a helpful reminder to all of us. Wishing you sweet dreams as
your amazing body regenerates. God's Word talks a great deal
about rest. We know God created the earth in six days, and
on the seventh day, He, Himself, rested. He established the

Sabbath as a day of rest: day seven of each week. No work was to be done on the Sabbath.

Today, Jesus has fulfilled all of the law, and now He is our rest.

> Come to Me, all you who labor and are heavy laden, and I will give you rest. Take My yoke upon you and learn from Me, for I am gentle and lowly in heart, and you will find rest for your souls.
>
> Matthew 11:28–29 (NKJV)

I believe God's design for us is to observe the sabbath, to work six days and rest on the seventh. I believe He made our bodies function most efficiently when we observe this principle.

Need for physical exercise

God made our bodies to move. He wants us to be strong physically, as well as mentally, and spiritually. All three are connected. Here is some advice on how to work out when it has been a while. Thinking about getting back in shape? You haven't worked out since when? Maybe you kept celebrating long after the holidays were over. Whatever you did or didn't do does not really matter because it's in the past. Today is the day for positive change. Where do you start?

In working with my fitness clients, I have learned several things that they have found helpful, and so will you. First things first. Do your thinking patterns need to be altered or at least shifted in such a way that your workouts become a priority in your weekly schedule? Now, be honest with yourself. Without the proper mindset, you are defeated before you start.

Secondly, choose something you like to do. My thing is dancing: ballet, modern, African, folk, you name it. It is a disciplinarian who will do this type of exercise alone, so find a class if you are not inspired to work by yourself. If you like running, go for it. Just don't try six miles the first day! You get the picture.

Finally, it is most important that you know and accept your current fitness level and start right where you are. Whatever the exercise, start there until you feel strong enough to go to the next level. It may mean less weight, fewer miles, or less area covered. One example is the Pilates leg circle. This exercise is done lying on one's back, making a large circle from the hip with a straight leg. A client of mine didn't have the strength to do a full circle with her leg extended, so I had her do a smaller circle until that was strong, and then I had her make the circle a little larger. She worked there for a few sessions and then went on to an even larger one. The result was that she was doing the full leg circle in a matter of weeks.

To recap:

1. Make your exercise program a priority.
2. Choose something you like to do.
3. Probably the most important, is to know your level and work there until you are strong enough to go to the next.

You will be back in shape in a healthy, injury-free way if youfollow these three tips.

Testimonies of Healing

My prayer for you, dear reader, is that you would know Jesus intimately and that your faith in healing would be increased. The following testimonies are from people I know personally. I have changed only their names.

Sarah

Seven years ago, I had a debilitating depression. I was unable to work or care for my family. I genuinely thought the entire world would be better if I were not a part of it. I had many thoughts of suicide and self-loathing. At my darkest moment, I cried out to God about how no one understood what I was going through. I heard a small, "I know." I clung to that small phrase. Jesus knows every pain and sorrow that I was experiencing. My faith in His atoning sacrifice brought me out of the darkness. I know it was by Him and through Him that I am here today.

Madeline

I've had a few healings, but the most recent was the Lord healing me from migraines. It was a few stages of healing throughout ten years. I was diagnosed with vestibular migraines and accompanying issues where I often struggled to function. After about 4 years, I had to leave my regular job since I only had about 1–3 hours of good time a day and could no longer drive. About a month after He called me into ministry, the Lord led me to a medication that allowed me a good 3–6 hours a day and drive again. I continued for a good while, treating the symptoms with medication until it was discontinued. The Lord held me through a miraculous month in July 2012 (another story of miracles entirely!). Then I found out I was pregnant a few months later and was led to a miracle answer in vitamin supplements. I was bedridden by the migraines at that point. Then, in April 2016, I was at a ministry meeting, and there was a call to prayer. One of the leaders in the team said she felt called to pray for me and my migraines. I was overwhelmed because literally a few minutes before, our event founder announced that she was diagnosed with cancer. I was sure that was the reason for a call to pray. Still, these prayer warriors and friends, including our friend with cancer and her father, laid hands on me and prayed for my healing. I noticed no difference that day, but the following day we went to church service with friends. That morning, worship was powerful, and there was a song playing that needed flags. So, our friend got them out and was down low worshipping with all she had. I thought, if she can do that with cancer, I surely can. So, I prayed and asked God not to let me have a migraine trigger when I leaned over to worship. It had always triggered migraines when I leaned over. I loved worshiping so freely. Then our friend shared the message for the service. It was on worship, which was no big surprise since she was a worship leader and teacher. I remember her specifically talking about how worship unlocks your healing and claimed in my heart healing for both her and myself. The rest of the day, God was faithful, and I did not get dizzy at all, not in the moment, and not on the drive. In fact, I didn't get dizzy the next day or the next: No vertigo, not even when I purposefully leaned over so I could play with my toddler daughter. I claimed the healing and told my husband I was healed. He watched me for over a week and noticed that I was not getting dizzy or having headaches when I leaned over for the first time in over ten years. I was down on the floor, playing with my daughter. I even went to a dance event and danced my heart out for the Lord for the first time. I was healed! I was telling everyone! A month later, my husband finally claimed it too and announced at a worship event, that I was truly healed. Our friend prompted me to share my testimony as an opening to the healing service that evening. God is amazing, and He is the healer!

Heather

I struggled with the fact that in my head and in my heart, I had done all I could do to release my father from the sexual abuse I had experienced from him from the ages of 4–7. He molested me and my two sisters and I had grown up hating him for that, disrespecting not just him but every male authority, distrusting authority in general, and putting up shields like obesity and a brazen personality to keep safe from further violation from men.

As a surrendered Christian at 20, I had longed to forgive him, but the little girl inside was so wounded that no matter how much I proclaimed him forgiven, even after he apologized sincerely in my early 30s, I still loathed or feared being in the same house with him or allowing my children near him. I felt terrible about this inability to release these things. It ate away at so much that should have been joy-

ful and beautiful in me. It affected my parenting, my rela-
tionships, certainly my relationship with my husband. At
38 I met an older woman who had written a book on how
the Lord healed her memories through Theophostic prayer.
Theophostic prayer is asking Jesus to reveal Himself in your
memories so that you may see them clearly. Where was Jesus
at the time of your abuse or trauma. She had had multiple
personalities brought together with the help of an Episcopal
priest who led her in prayer. I asked her if she would pray
with me because I was so ready to be free of this burden. She
and I met for several weeks and each time we concentrated
on only one memory. Once I had that memory fully established in my mind we went to prayer, asking Jesus to reveal
Himself to me in the prayer. He walked right into that scene,
picked up my little 6 or 7-year-old self, and I wrapped my
legs around his waist. He held me tight in a hug I could feel,
not just see. He sent my daddy out of the room, saying "I will
deal with you later", and then stood there holding me, calm-
ing me, and saying, "Heather, you are mine. You have always
been mine. You will always be mine. What another does to
you they do to me. Your daddy is not well. I will fix him; you
don't have to do that. He is my problem, not yours. You just
rest and hold on to me. I've got you." Clear as day, these are
now my memories (I told you only one; they were all different, but this one was the strongest) and memory by memory,
I was fully healed. Since that time no thoughts of bitterness,
fear, anger or loathing have entered my mind toward this
man, only compassion and pity. Sure, I got impatient from
time to time with him, but only about present circumstances.
When he was on his death bed, I reminded him of Christ's
suffering and his redeeming love and grace. I ministered to
my father as best I could in the years following my healing,
and while he struggled to receive grace, struggled to believe,

he admitted that this grace shown to him through me and the other Christians in his life was real and convincing. I am at peace that he is truly "God's problem" and that whatever the Lord chooses to do with any soul is perfect and right.

Tamika

I was healed of inherited heart problems when I was a young adult. These heart problems started as a teenager. I had tachycardia and mitral valve prolapse. Most of the women in my family have varying degrees of these heart issues. I had the worst. I was in and out of the hospital and later put on medication of eight pills a day. The Lord miraculously healed me one night in my living room. I later received medical documentation that the pre-existing heart problems were no longer present! I have been free ever since!

Anna

From the ages of 17–21, I was in an emotionally abusive relationship. I was young and ignorant. I thought it was love. Then I found out I was pregnant, and the you-know-what hit the fan. I knew I couldn't raise that child in an abusive relationship. Instead of leaving, I acted out. I did things I was not proud of, but I got the desired effect. He violently left me. Alone, broken, and scared, I gave the baby up for adoption. I was in no place to take care of myself, let alone a child. My mind was still warped by the abuse, and my heart broke from what I thought was a lost love. Abortion was never a choice. That child has a purpose. But losing him broke me further.

Once the child was placed, my life became self-destructive. I was partying and drinking and partaking in the sins of skin. I was also cutting myself, hoping I would have the courage to press down. I was numb. I felt nothing. I never smiled, or cried, or laughed, or found joy in anything. My life was a black hole, sucking the light out of it with reckless abandon. I wanted it to end. My days were filled with self-loathing, my nights filled with ghost cries of my lost child. My soul was withering. I knew I couldn't commit suicide, so I sought things that would end me.

At 24, the devil took hold, and I felt it. It was cold desperation. I was ready to die. I just had to find a way to do it that wouldn't leave a mess for my mother to clean up. I walked outside. I walked toward the busy street, and I waited for the right car. I saw it. I took a step forward, but something snatched my spine.

"Are you sure?" someone whispered.

"No." I said. "I just want the pain to stop." I felt warmth flood through me, chasing away the cold fingers of Satan.

I turned around and walked home. I got on my hands and knees, my head hung low, and said, "Daddy? Papa! Dada! I'm sorry. I can't do this alone. I need you. Without you I will die and I don't want to die. But I can't live without you. Please, Papa, please take it. It's yours. I give myself to you."

Silence at first. Then, "There is one more thing." It was like a whisper.

I looked up, my stubborn heart on the warpath. "Get out Satan! My soul belongs to Jesus. My heart belongs to my Daddy. And you can't have me, anymore!"

For the first time in three years, I felt again. It was instant. No waiting. No more trials. My Father had taken away my pain. There was still a little residual pain. I still missed that baby. But I could function. I could breathe. The emotional and mental abuse were gone. It took years still to cope with losing the child. But I was human again, not just a shell. I smiled again. I laughed and loved again. And to this day, my heart still belongs with Jesus.

I was raised a Christian. And I always believed. But I never felt God in my life. However, since then, I feel Him all the time. I'm not the best I can be yet, but I know my Father is always fighting along my side, keeping me grounded and reminding me that I belong to Him. Forever.

I haven't shared this story with many people. But I felt like it was time. So, there it is: How my Daddy saved my life, again.

Marianna

I had severe sinus headaches in the late 80s. After meds failed, the doctor prescribed surgery. Instead, I prayed, and my late dad, who was also my pastor, laid hands on me in the mighty name of Jesus Christ, and I was instantly healed! I have been free of sinusitis and its symptoms ever since! Many others received healing when my late dad laid hands on them in the name of Jesus Christ.

Work it Out!

"I sought the LORD, and he heard me, and delivered me from all my fears" (Psalm 34:4, NKJV). As you continue in your journey toward wholeness, consider these things:

1.   First and foremost, do you belong to Jesus? I know I keep bringing this up, but it is the bottom line.
        Yes, or no?

2.   Are you sure?
        Yes, or no?

3.   Why?

_____

_____

_____

_____

_____

4.   What scriptures convince you of this?

_____

_____

_____

_____

_____

5. Have You been baptized in the Holy Spirit?
    Yes or no?

6. How do you know this?

    _____

    _____

    _____

    _____

    _____

7. Give scriptures for your answer.

    _____

    _____

    _____

    _____

    _____

8. What things in your body, mind, and spirit do you need
    to **drop from** your life?

    _____

    _____

    _____

    _____

    _____

9. What is your plan of action?

    _____

    _____

    _____

    _____

10. What things in your body, mind, and spirit do you need to add to your life?

_____

_____

_____

_____

_____

11. What support systems do you need?

_____

_____

_____

_____

12. What support systems do you have in place?

_____

_____

_____

_____

13. Your prayers:

_____

_____

_____

_____

14. Answers to your prayers:

_____

_____

_____

_____

_____

15. Affirmations and confessions based on scripture:

_____

_____

_____

_____

_____

16. Additional thoughts and notes:

_____

_____

_____

_____

_____

Bibliography

Strong, J. 1890. *Strong's exhaustive concordance of the Bible.* Abingdon Press.

Vilhauer, J. "Why Ghosting Hurts so Much," November 27, 2015. https://www.psychologytoday.com/us/blog/living-forward/201511/why-ghosting-hurts-so-much.

About the Author

Donna Martelli was determined to be a dancer, and a good one at that, by the sweet age of ten. Her classical ballet study began with one class a week and progressed, by her mid-teens, to six days a week. During her senior year in high school, she danced many leading roles in major ballets, including Swan Lake, Ondine, and original works. What happened next was amazing. She was selected as one of eight girls from over two hundred and fifty candidates to be a trainee in the Harkness

Ballet. Anyone who knows ballet will recognize her teachers' names: Donald Sadlier, George Skibine, Marjorie Tallchief, Vera Volkova, Leon Fokine, Alvin Ailey, Patricia Wilde, and Stewart Hodes, to name a few. It was a God set-up: they were the best teachers in the entire world at that time.

Besides classes in ballet and modern dance, she studied Music Theory, Labanotation, Character Dance, Choreography, Anatomy, and many other related subjects.

Seven months into the trainee program, she was asked to join The Harkness Ballet. She toured Europe and North Africa, dancing various parts in many ballets utilizing ballet, modern, and jazz dance techniques.

Years later, she met Jesus and laid dance down, only to have Him bring it back to her in a new and sanctified way. Now, Donna loves teaching those who desire to dance for the Lord. She is also passionate about teaching the healing aspects of dance. Additionally, she is a certified personal trainer and certified Pilates instructor, and a staff member at LivRite Fitness, Indianapolis, Indiana. She offers barre classes, personal training sessions, resistance and strength training lessons, classes in ballet fit, Pilates, and many other fitness training classes to any age, regardless of experience.

She offers quality training DVDs as well as a certification in Christian dance. For more information, see www. donnamartelli.com, www.beautiful-feet.org.

Thank you, the end.